Journal of a Lonely Man

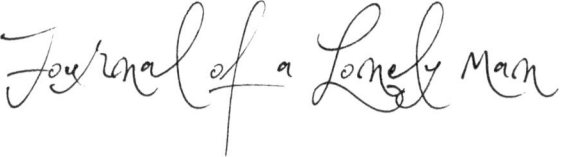

Calvin Warden II

Columbus, Ohio

This book is a work of fiction. The names, characters and events in this book are the products of the author's imagination or are used fictitiously. Any similarity to real persons living or dead is coincidental and not intended by the author.

The views and opinions expressed in this book are solely those of the author and do not reflect the views or opinions of Gatekeeper Press. Gatekeeper Press is not to be held responsible for and expressly disclaims responsibility of the content herein.

Journal of a Lonely Man: Poetry

Published by Gatekeeper Press
2167 Stringtown Rd, Suite 109
Columbus, OH 43123-2989
www.GatekeeperPress.com

Copyright © 2020 by Calvin Warden II
All rights reserved. Neither this book, nor any parts within it may be sold or reproduced in any form or by any electronic or mechanical means, including information storage and retrieval systems, without permission in writing from the author. The only exception is by a reviewer, who may quote short excerpts in a review.

Library of Congress Control Number: 2020950060
ISBN (paperback): 9781662906152
eISBN: 9781662906169

Contents

Echoes of Love	10
Healer's Lament	11
Awakening	12
You	13
Free as a Bird	14
But Now	15
Together	16
Bad Memories	17
The Fight	18
Look into my Eyes	19
Poem of Poetry	21
The Searcher	22
Silent Screams	23
Flashback	24
Reality	25
The Lonesome King	26
End?	27
Something More	28
Reach	29
Two Alone, Two Are One	31
Depression	32
I'm Fine	33
Beacon	35

You Should Know	36
All In All	37
Lost Road	38
Beauty Within	39
Cleansing Rain	40
We Are	41
Regret	42
New Paths	43
By Any Other Name	44
Weathering The Storm	45
The Monster, I	46
Searching	47
Real/Illusion	49
Moonlit Eyes	50
Up Ahead	51
Here	52
Darkened Spell	53
Standing	55
Weary Bones	57
Confusion	58
For All Of Us	59
One To Speak	60
Warning Signs	61
Unspoken Words	62
The Mix Of Love and Life	63
Looking to the Moon	64

So Tell Me Stranger	67
Mental Anguish	69
My Mental Anguish	71
Truth About Love	72
Fluid Time	73
Shadows Smiles	74
Monsters Of Old	75
Pushed To The Edge	76
Fist Of Tears	77
This I Do	78
Warmth	79
Poet's Eyes	80
Dark World	81
Moon Fire	83
Times Gift	84
The Heart's Rhythm	85
Nothing is Trivial	87
Be Free	88
Hidden Charm	89
Faded Lines	90
Think	91
Spread Truth	93
The Artist	94
Watching and Waiting	95
In The Sky	96
Free But Alone	97

Sixteen	98
In Search Of Her	99
All in a Dream	100
Protector's Soul	101
The Fool, Me	102
The Fool Within	103
Powerful Love	104
Empty Terror	105
Inside These Walls	106
Dream	107
Dreamland	108
Holding in a Dream	109
Blind Path	110
Part Of You	111
Isolation Destroys	112
To Whom It May Concern	113
In The Name Of Friendship	114
I've Seen	115
Fear	116
Don't Judge Me	117
Sometimes A Man Can Bleed	118
Understand Me	119
Remember Me	120
Stand Together	121
Summer's Tears	122
Rising Sun	123

Journal of a Lonely Man

by
Calvin Warden II

I dedicate this book to my kids, family, and friends.
Those of past, present, and future. I love you all.
And a special thank you to you, the reader.

Echoes of Love

I was made for you
You know I'm not wrong
It's like you're the singer
And I'm your song
Now here is the truth
You still run and hide
You're simply afraid
Of the feelings deep inside
So for now I sit here
Alone in the pouring rain
Not understanding why
I have to hide this pain
Soon the time will come
And I know you'll see
I am made for you
As you are made for me

Healer's Lament

A healer's heart feels your pain
Giving you its all to feel whole again.
Steadily seeking out your sorrow
Hoping to build you a better tomorrow.
Not caring what happens to me
Just so long as you're happy and free.
I might not always do what's right
But I want to help you through the night.
So just lay down and get some rest
'Cause when I'm with you, I'm at my best.

Awakening

I asked her her name
She didn't reply
Awaken

I asked her who she was
She didn't know
Awaken

I asked her about love
She seemed so lost
Awaken

I told her to look inside
She began to think
Awaken Awaken

I told her to just be her
She started to smile
Awaken Awaken

I told her I love her
She now loves her too
Awaken Awoken

Calvin Warden II

You

I began dancing with my demons
As I lost my way so long ago.
Then she came into my life
And my demons ran away.
Now I feel so alone and empty
Without the torture to my soul.
Searching for long gone peace
Holding my angel's hand again.
But why do I feel so alone
Like I'm spinning through space.
Wandering never to seen again
To ever be in another's embrace.
I don't understand why this has come
Or even what I'm now to do.
You have always been within reach
And yet far beyond my grasp.
Can't you understand this as I do
And stop resisting the truth.
You know it as well as I do
The answer had always been you.

Free as a Bird

The songbird sings its lonely song
As I sit and listen to the traffic
The mockingbird sings a forgotten song
As I hide in a condemned building
The eagle screams its battle cry
As I watch the static on the TV
The crow cries its warming caw
As I see the sirens fly by
The hummingbird wisps as it floats aloft
As I slowly climb the stairs
The falcon spies its next meal
As I reach the roof so high
The owl asks its unanswered question
As I take the step to be free
The swallows eggs begin to hatch
As I soar through the sky at last

But Now

Once we were as close as can be
Now we don't even talk at all
You were always by my side
Now I never get to see you smile
We were the best of friends
Now you never mention my name
No one knew more about me
Now you don't even recognize me
I was told you'd never leave me
Now I always sit alone... alone

Together

She whispered that she loves me
Not knowing that she was saving me
She was suffering her own battles
So I offered myself as her armor
She pulled me out of endless darkness
I showed her how to center herself
She reminds me to help myself
And I give to her my everything
She shines even in the darkest night
My hand is always there to help her up
She is the one I've been searching for
Finally she has been given her voice

Bad Memories

All I have are empty dreams.
Hopeless fate or so it seems.
To say I live would be a lie.
But nor do I want to die.
For I have long lost my friend.
My soul no longer will mend.
My heart is broken and lonely.
Since all have left me to be.
Never again shall I have rest.
Waking up hoping for the best.
But then she will never realize.
That I have never told her lies.
Never will she believe the cost.
Because now I am forever lost.
All I wanted was to be a friend.
Will this torment ever end?

The Fight

I thought you were sent from above
My final love
But then I fell
And I realised that you were from Hell
You promised that you'd remain true
But now I'm blue
Killed by glance
You never gave me a real chance
Your actions I still can not condone
You left me alone
I don't know why
But you have left me alone to die
Yet I know I'm stronger than you think
I refuse to sink
Nothing to do
And yet I know my life is not through

Look into my Eyes

I look into her eyes
   As green as jade or
   As blue as the clear sky
I listen to her heart beat
   As deep as a bass drum
   As light as an angels horn
I hear her gentle voice
   As load as a lions roar
   As soothing as a gentle summers rain
I embrace you in my arms
   As worlds collide
   As stars fall

Journal of a Lonely Man

I wade through my emotions
   As I love you
   As I cower from you
I dream of you
   As the sun raises
   As our lives begin
I care deeply for you
   As though we are one
   As our souls combine
You look me in the eyes
   And you know I'm true
And you feel it too

Poem of Poetry

The blank page waits to be filled
The pen waits to spill its blood
The words that swim around my head
Are just waiting to be set free
And then the pen begins to cry
And the blank page forever is ruined
And the words are no longer held back
Never again shall the truth be held back
The pen is flurry with raw emotion
The page cries out in relief
The emotional dam finally destroyed
And the world is set free again

The Searcher

Empty promises and broken dreams
Following your heart is harder than it seems
In search of everlasting love
To many wrong paths lie before me
My mind says it's not meant to be
That love is no longer there for me
But I keep trudging toward my goal
Really what else could I do
These feelings keep swelling up inside
As if they are trying to bury me
Preventing a future I can no longer see
But in truth what does it all mean
Is there really more to this existence
More than broken promises and empty dreams

Silent Screams

I hide from the sandman
As he fights me for sleep
While it's the rest I need
It's my dreams that creep
Visions of you are killing me
Are these memories true
Were you ever real
Or just make believe
Product of isolation
Creation of my own
My own tormention
A ravenous hallucination
Proof of my damnation
You are the one that is there
Never releasing your grip
Ripping me to shreds
Shattering me to pieces
I scream so loud and long
Never to be heard again
Will anyone break the silence

Flashback

I lay awake and watch my lover sleep
So far away and still within arms reach
I wish I could turn back time to regain what
I've lost
But what would I achieve and what would
be the cost
I know I love her and this is true
But I'm lost and I don't know what to do
How can I be with you and still feel
so alone
Where is the love you said you have for me
Forever must be shorter than I remember
I must be stupid for feeling this way
Why can't I shake the love that I have
I wish I could see in your heart
and know for sure
Do you love me anymore because
I love you

Calvin Warden II

Reality

Somewhere along the way
My life has gone astray
But don't you shed a tear
Because I have no fear
I know in my heart I'm trying
For the life I want I keep fighting

The Lonesome King

The minstrel plays his best tunes
And the jester tells his best jokes
Still the king does not smile.
The knights protect the land
And the peasants toil in field
Still the king ponders

.

The wizards performed his magic
And the alchemist mixes a potion
Still the king doesn't notice.
The rogue is plundering the treasure
And the bar room is a total brawl
Still the king remains unaware.
The guilds men practice their craft
And the merchants sell their wares
Still the king always feels alone.
The kingdom has lasting peace
And all within praise his rule
Still the king searches for his queen.
The passage of time marches on
And yet my heart remains pure
Still the king... Still I sit alone.

End?

The words began to flow into my mind
Like water flowing over Angel Falls
Distractions
Then silence
The story no longer comes out
Words fresh in thought vanished
Who stole my words
What is to come of the blank pages
My muse had abandoned me
Stories are left unfinished
I don't see what is to happen next
How will it all...

Something More

The eyes of an angel are upon me
Watching me during lonely nights
Protecting me throughout the day
Showing herself when need be
I know my angel watches me
And I know that should be enough
But I still search for more
I need my earthly mate in love
In my heart, mind, and my arms
I still crave for earthly love
Needing her true love forever

Reach

I found myself lost in thought
Trapped in my poisonous past
Searching for my way home
Trying to find that tranquil place
But I can't find a way out of here
There must be some spell to use
But I don't know this magic
And I've exhausted my search
Yet I continue this journey
Guided by my shining star
So why do I keep moving along
Because I know life is precious
Yes it can be a real challenge
When your energy stops flowing

Journal of a Lonely Man

And you're always seeking love
Knowing that cupid is cruel
So instead you build walls
And keep your heart guarded
But eventually those walls will fall
And the clock will tick along
And you may not want it
But this doesn't make you weak
And letting someone in well...
That does make you breakable
But you need to remember this
That love is always a gift
So don't be afraid to try
And reach for that slice of life

Two Alone, Two Are One

I awaken to her silent screams,
As she cried alone in the dark,
Downing in emotional pain.
I feel as though she were here,
But not even knowing who she is,
Maybe even a million miles away.
I want to rear her distress,
Let her know that she's not alone,
Yet I don't know how to do that.
I hope she know that I'm here for her,
Ready to share her pain,
As I myself sit and cry alone.

Depression

It's a bright beautiful day
And I sit alone in the dark.
I have so many things to do
And yet no desire to do them.
Family and friends reach out
And yet I always feel so alone.
The art that I've always loved
Has lost its luster and draw.
My words that once flowed free
Has become forced and it shows.
The joys I once had with little things
Has disappeared and began to hide.
So what does this mean to me
And those that I care about?
What will it take to revitalize
And what will I have lost?
How will I ever be me once again
And who will still be by my side?

I'm Fine

I tell them I'm fine
They know it's a lie

Sigh

They know that sometimes wrong
But they don't know the cause

Sigh

They can see the pain
Yet not every see the scars

Sigh

Even surrounded by people
I remain oh so alone

Journal of a Lonely Man

Sigh

This burden is mine alone
And I see it reflect in your eyes

Sigh

Why do I continue to fight
When my misery I spread

Sigh

Only I can eliminate this dread
Free myself from this torture

Sigh

So when you ask me how I am
I will lie and say I'm fine

Beacon

It's been a long time now
And yet I still struggle
Searching for lost love
I seem to be all alone
But I know this is not true
Because I always see you
But I know not who you are
For we have never met
And yet this seems to be the way
You are always watching me
And I'm always seeking you
So why are you so hard to find
Always hiding from my love
You're hiding in the shadows
Hiding from love's true light
A light that is pure and complement
When you're ready to leave the dark
Just follow the warm light's glow

You Should Know

He beat you down once again
She destroyed your world
You are playing the fool
You're believing all the lies
Always being led astray
Following the simplest path
Leading to the familiar pain
Ignoring those who try to help
Not seeing what's there
Never hearing the truth
Knowing what you know
You are worth so much more.

Calvin Warden II

All In All

Within me lives all those who came before
Not just those of shared blood lines
But everything that has ever been
Even the earth beneath my feet
Yet there is still more within me
For everything in the sky as well
The sun, moon, and the stars
Knowledge and wisdom forgotten
Tales that have never been told
Worlds born that are now gone
So when you look at me
Remember there is then you see.

Lost Road

You said you'd love me forever
That we would always be as one
Somewhere along the way you turned
And I went to follow your love
But you were already gone
So now I stand alone
In the middle of the road
So many people passing by
None seem to notice
Lost in their own worlds
Not caring about ours
So where did it all go wrong
Was I chasing the moon
While you were chasing the stars
I believed we were on the same path
But were we just in passing lanes
Watching the same scene
Dreaming the same dream
Or are we meant to be together
Will our paths collide again
This I need to know
Because I'll always love you

Beauty Within

As I stare into her eyes our world
become clear
The beauty in all things that surround us
The love in everything we do
and have done
The joy we share with all that we meet
The healing glow that we now cast out
The growth of something more than just us
The two that that have managed to change
The one that they have somehow become
The depth of understanding imperfection
The acceptance of one's self and others
As I stare into her eyes everything
is beautiful

Cleansing Rain

Standing in the open I face the rain
Welcoming its cool embrace
As it washes away all my worries
And my tears just fade away
Memories are now being blurred
As the the clouds fall down on me
The rains bring me peace again
But is the rain really the reason
Opening my eyes it's all clear
It's not the rain falling from above
But you standing next to me
Standing lovingly hand in hand

We Are

I find myself buried in darkness
Searching for any sign of light
So lost in this vast emptiness
Grasping just to feel anything
What is this place so strange
So void of all things real
It leaves my senses wanting
As I find myself drifting away
Can there truly be nothing
Absolutely no one to be found
But then I feel a strange warmth
And suddenly I know you're there
And you are all I'll ever need
Because alone we are complete
But together we are so much more
So even when apart the magic flows

Regret

Your love kept me aloft for years
Now I'm grounded filled with sorrow
My world has flooded with my own tears
Sitting alone I wait for a better tomorrow
I'm wondering what I should do now
Questioning how did I drive you away
I love you still but don't know how
Will we be together again some day
You tell me I did nothing wrong
Then why did you have to leave
Do you no longer believe our song
Fine then leave me here to grieve
I don't know who I am anymore
Nor do I know where I belong
I'm in a lot of pain but I am not sore
To rebuild my would I now say so long.

New Paths

Traveling down the road well know
I never see anything new
So what is this before me
A path hidden in obscurity
Do I dare very from my path
Will my strength see me to the end
What awaits me if I leave this road
Wonders untold never before seen
Worlds never meant to exist
Decisions need to be made now
As I take a step without thought
And behold it all becomes...

By Any Other Name

Who's the one with the white rose
Standing alone in the rain
Attempting to hide their tears
And let the pain slowly wash away

Who's the one with the yellow rose
Running and holding hands again
Sharing their life with their friend

Who's the one with the red rose
So passionately filled with love

Who's the one with the wilted rose

Weathering The Storm

I found you sitting alone in the rain
As you were pretending not to cry
The rain washing the tears away
But not removing the pain in your eyes
I offer you a hand to help you up
But you turn me down for now
You are comfortable in the rain
Hiding yourself from the world
You tell me you're happy where you are
But I know you're suffering in pain
I realize that you made yourself weak
Too weary to move but not to speak
So I sit next to you in this downpour
And I lend to you my strength
A smile now begins slowly show
And I whisper oh so softly to you
There's a reason I'm in the rain too

The Monster, I

The monster lumbers through the night
Hiding from those that he needs
Those who see him know not what to do
Or what it is that they have seen
What is it that they all so afraid of
The monster is afraid of being hurt
Everyone else is afraid of the monster
So what is there to really fear
Is the monster really all that scary
Why is it you run away in fear
Without the slightest bit of understanding
Do you even know what the monster seeks
No I don't believe you ever have
No one has ever taken the time try
To try and find the truth that lies within
So the monster continues alone
Hiding within the dark in pain
Hiding his general should
Hardening his heart within stone
And forever searching for love

Searching

I need to be grounded upon this earthly sphere
Because this is where my temporal body resides
And yet my soul cries out to be set free
Longing for an adventure lost in love
But is that really the way to go lost and alone
Struggling to find that which does not exist
The love of another is an eternal quest
But the love I have to give is forever flowing
A never ending rain falling over this mortal ball of dirt
Healing all that have the courage to accept it

But where and when will this all end
I know the fountain cannot continue
forever
Not even this soul can survive without
sustenance
With so much to give asking so little
in return
Confused, lost, and wandering in the
clouds a high
Trapped alone in the darkness below
So where am I in this mess that I now lie
Trying to find my peace and love lost
Just trying to find that which is needed
Achieving that believed to be only fantasy

Real Illusion

Love is an illusion
But pain oh so real
Charging down a dream
Stuck in this reality
Turning this way and that
Only to be standing still
I see you everywhere
But then you're not real
Just a longing desire
To feel that connection
One that once was
But will never be again
So here I still stand
Searching now
Because I still believe
In this crazy dream
The illusion called love

Moonlit Eyes

Standing in the light of the moon
I realized that I was not alone
I feel the eyes that set upon me
But to whom do they belong
A fallen star or angel from above
Or simply my mind running wild
Is this just wishful thinking
Dreams of a broken heart
Or are these feelings real
I'm overwhelmed by emotions
As my journey comes to an end
Still standing in the moon's glow

Up Ahead

Always alone I continue on
Racing towards unknown love
Not sure where the path leads
Or who will join along the way
But I'm ready for the journey
An adventure in love and joy
I know there will be perils
And work yet to be done
But at journey's end
It will be worth it all
Just to be with the real one

Here

I was held together by scars and bandages
And countless pains that you'll never know
Yet I hide behind no mask of any kind
Always wearing my heart on my sleeve
Sharing my love with all the world to see
Living life the best way that I know how
Trying to make the world smile again
Bringing others into my own peace
And sheltering them from the storm
I do all this with the greatest of ease
But I still wish that love would find me

Darkened Spell

What happened when I looked in your eyes
Was it then that I was bewitched by you
That long distance memory ago
Before I even really got to know you
That sudden and instant connection
I knew things would never be the same
My story has forever been changed
And there would never be me without you
No matter where you are I always feel
I always felt when you had need of me
Just to be left behind once again
I wish to be released from this spell
Wanting to bask in the sun again
Instead of hidden in the shadows of you heart

Journal of a Lonely Man

But we both know that is too late for that
Because your spell has set into me
And I can no longer be set free
I forever more belong to you
But no more to you will I run in ruin
Because once again my eyes see
And now my life will run wild
As I take my leave of you now
My new struggle will begin

Calvin Warden II

Lying awake in the field as the rain pours down on me
Drowning in the memories that I don't want to see
Reliving the pain that was released unto the world
As if I were slashed by a thousand swords or more
Feeling like a shark in the ocean that forgot how to swim
Struggling to keep the slightest grip on this new reality

But I know that you are there watching me for now
Just waiting to step up and offer yourself to me
To give me the shelter that I so desperately need
For the chance to raise up and finally catch my breath
To be free the chaos and being balance to the world
But for now I start by simply standing on my own

Weary Bones

I stand before you battered and bruised
Struggling just to keep my feet
Been knocked down time after time
But I have always pulled myself up
Now my strength is beginning to wane
Fighting just to keep going on
Only to fall further and further behind
Stumbling with every step I take
Even though I know I'm not done
I can no longer stand on my own
So for now I'll just sit where I am
And wait as time slowly passes by
As my weary starts to wander
And my aching heart begins to slow
The day now draws to a lonely end
As I try my hardest to find my feet once again

Confusion

Is this fantasy or reality
It has to be one or the other
At least that's what they say
But is that really the case
Either nightmare or dream
But there is a deeper truth
One that is easy to see
There is often a choice
Something that lies between
The truth of the matter is
We are living in both
In a realm that lies beyond
And I'm never looking back
Now that the truth is clear

For All of Us

For lovers come and gone
And those who chase the sun
I write my words for all of you
Dreamers of tomorrow's dawn
Those hiding beneath the moon
I write my words for all of you
Everyone both lost and found
All my family and friends
I write my words for all of you
But then is this really true
Because I believe in reality
I write my words only for me
Yes I share everything you
And I'm glad you all can enjoy
So maybe I write my words…

One To Speak

I once believed love was easy
Just simply follow your heart
And let it lead you to joy
But now I know that it's more
And I find it hard to ignore
It's often hard work
And many times unwanted
Causing deep pain within
Does that mean don't try
Or that you should give up
And let your heart turn cold
Well this is my reply
I will not let you give up
And I'm here to remind you
Love is worth the fight

Calvin Warden II

I've read the signs,
I've ignored them till now,
They said I was (in love),
I told the no (I didn't believe them),
But this problem I can't ignore anymore,
I've got to tell the truth (I am in love),
To whom I can't say,
But maybe someday,
Far away,
If only she's with me.

Unspoken Words

My unspoken words,
The mix of love and truth,
The spoken words,
Hide all that I feel,
My love for her is real,
The way she knows,
    The way I write,
        L-O-V-E.

The Mix Of Love and Life

The world is a dark and shallow place,
Everyone wears a frown on their face.
The peace of life to be taken from me,
This I give so you can be free.
The love I once knew, was true,
But now my love life is through.
The Angel I once loved,
Now flies like a dove.
This pain we shared,
For nothing we feared.
She left me and went to the sky,
I never thought I'd be the one to cry.

Looking to the Moon

I find myself lost and alone
Midnight looking up to the sky
Searching for the moon that is gone
"What are you looking for?"
A voice from nowhere asks
"Looking for my lost love."
I slowly say as my reply
Then the mystery voice says
"So why is it that you look to the sky?"
My voice is now only wavering
"She said let the moon be your guide."
And now the unknown begins to cry
So I don't know what to say now
my voice now only a whisper
"Why is it that now you cry?"
Between the sobs the voice replies
"No one ever looks to me for love."
So now in the darkness we sit
And together we now cry as one

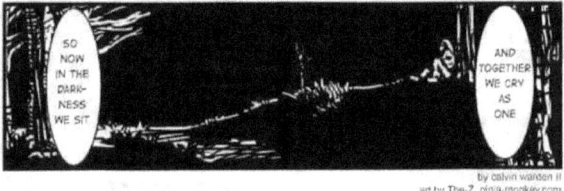

So Tell Me Stranger

So tell me stranger what's your name,
So tell me stranger what's your fame,
So tell me stranger what's your game,

What does it take to get in your game,
What does it take to find your fame,
What does it take to say your name,

Can you tell me your name,
Can you let me on on your fame,
Can you explain your game,

Journal of a Lonely Man

Do you know your game,
Do you know your fame,
Do you even know your name,

Should I find your game,
Should I give you fame,
Should I tell you your name,

Should I just let you play,
So tell me stranger it's really up to you,
Is this part of your game (fame)?

Mental Anguish

The soul is set free
    While encased by thought
The mind tried to fly to the sun
    Without burning its wings
Instead flies to the sea
    Falls in and drowns
And if the dam breaks open
    Many years too soon
We'll have to study lovers and fighters
    And the risks they take in the other
side of life
The lovely man cries for love
    But there's no one to reply

Mental anguish and self-inflicted pain
    But who's left to blame
Do you want change to last
    'cause the future lies in the past
The walls around us start to crumble
    That will make the world fall and stumble
Into its grave
    It wants to pray
We'll have to change our days
    And the days are on their way
It's time for me to go
    Straight to the show

My Mental Anguish

I shared my life with her,
Her thoughts she hid from me,
She left me for another,
Another left her to be,
Her pain she does not feel,
For it's her pain that I steal,
The deep pain tries to kill her,
Pain she tries not to feel,
The daze on which she cries,
For her love has told her lies,
She left me here to cry,
With my life she will fly,
I now know she'll never be,
Never be in love with me,
To me she was cruel,
She treated me like a fool,
I love her with all my heart,
She made my world fall apart,
Now their love is through,
But our friendship is still true.

Truth About Love

To love is to live,
To live is to love,
To have love is life,
To have none is death,
If you want you have hope,
If you don't care,
   you don't love,
I love, and I share,
I live, and I'll die,
I teach, and I take,
I love, and I freak.

Calvin Warden II

Fluid Time

I face the onslaught of the past
Drowning in memories of old
Standing at tomorrow's door
But always looking behind
Searching for a better future
Trying to make it through the day
Wandering and wondering
Questioning many choices
But not living with regret
Though trying to catch my breath
Hanging myself with a sentimental noose
Forgetting that I'm living today
I need to escape my past
And stop looking to the future
So that I can just breath.

Shadows Smile

I step from the shadows into the light
Only to see the shadows smile
Straddling reality and a dream
Trying to see through the darkness
Searching for that one wish
That of love to show me the way
Back to feelings long lost
Something to make me feel again
To not feel so numb inside
So now I stand here in the sun
Just trying to find my way once again
Heading down this forgotten path
Seeking the love that lies ahead
And leaving all the darkness behind

Calvin Warden II

Monsters Of Old

The monsters that keep me awake
Are memories of you
Always fighting to keep the pain away
Not knowing what to do
Protecting you the only way I know
As I walk next to you
But you never even noticed me
Never even had a clue
Ignoring me was so easy those days
Never thinking of us two
But now I've gone and turned away
It was the only thing to do
I'm still searching for something real
And you, something new
But the worst thing keeping me awake
And you know it's true
Is not a memory but something else
I'll never stop loving you

Pushed To The Edge

The world has pushed me to the limit
Forcing me to stand on the cliff's edge
And you stand there waiting
Just hoping to watch me fall
But I'm here to tell you not to wait
Because a fall is not in store
Even if you push and shove me
I'll continue to stand strong
As weak and weary as I may be
My resolve is always that much more
So you just watch as the cliff crumbles
But watch me as I begin to soar

Fist Of Tears

Voices of silence scream out loud
As echoes verberate in my head
Tears fall from hands filled with sorrow
And a heart so full of emptiness
Wondering what I have done wrong
And why I deserve all this pain
But then it all becomes clear to me
That this is no fault of mine
So I must continue through
To see the joy on the other side
Wishing for my smile to return
And always dreaming of you

This I Do

You shut me out
But I break through
I can see the truth
Through the fake smile
And hollow laughs
Feel the pain there
Hidden from the world
That others cannot see
Trying to push me away
Protect me you say
Yet here I stand
Fighting by your side
Despite my own pain
I'll lift you up
And set you free again
Knowing the word is right
Once again

Warmth

The shadows dance with ghosts
As my soul tries to break free
Pain and sorrow weighing it down
In this expanse of loneliness
But I keep trudging through
Knowing this can't go on forever
As I search for the faint light
Breaking through the veil of darkness
So I can find love's guide
And feel its warm embrace
So why am I sitting in sorrow
Well I'm just regaining my strength

Poet's Eyes

I stand by and watch silently
As I myself put pen to page
The poet's words begin to flow
As the pen dances with glee
Jumping with reckless abandon
Leaving behind its broken trail
The letters join together as one
And the words form their line
All guided by the unknown
Never stopping till the poem is done
Stepping back I see the work
Knowing not its origins
Or where the words come from
Silenced by what's upon the page
And realizing that work is mine

Dark World

Where were you when gravity failed
And the stars began to fall
The world was in turmoil
And all love forgotten
Did you hear your name in the wind
See your reflection in the sea
Understand the pain below
As the Earth cried out loud
Time had lost all meaning
And emotions were crossed
As everything floated away
I stood firm and alone
Crying out your name once more
Searching everywhere for you

Journal of a Lonely Man

Just to hold you again
Just to feel your love
To let you know I care
And I never stopped searching
Now alone in this desolate world
Memories are all that remain
With my heart full of love
But no one to give it to
I'm forever chasing shadows
So lost and forgotten
As I think nevermore
What is that which I see
Another illusion or maybe
Someone has come to rescue me

Moon Fire

We wander through the woods
Taking in nature's wilds
Watching as the moon rises
Gathering around our camp
Trading tales and stories
Reconnecting with each other
And with nature itself
Gathering around the fire
And listening to one another
Along with nature's song
Under the stars above
Sitting down all together
Warmed by the the moon's glow

Times Gift

Time has come and gone
Taking with it my youth
Leaving aches and pain
And wisdom untold
I see things differently
But now I feel free
It has taken a long time
But finally I'm me
It is not good or bad
It's just so I am
And I accept it all
My strength and flaws
Not regretting the past
Or worrying of the future
Just taking it as it comes
I know it's not always easy
But everyone need to do this
Be true to who you are
And the rest will fall in place

The Heart's Rhythm

I found my love so true
She was standing there alone
Bathed in total moon light
She knows I'm standing there
And yet she says nothing
Nothing at all to me
She begins to move slowly
Dancing around the fire
To an unheard rhythm
A beat driving her body
Moving with such grace
And a freedom unbound
She knows I'm watching
As she smiles happily

Journal of a Lonely Man

Listening to silent music
Never looking at me
She reaches out
Pulling me toward her
Without a single touch
I didn't know she did it
But now I'm dancing too
Smiling to be with her
And hearing the beat
Together we dance
We smile
We sing
We love

Nothing is Trivial

The world has knocked me down
And I lay battered and bruised
As people just step over me
Never giving a glance my way
But that is their problem
Because I will rise again
Remembering who was with me
And those who stood in my way
I bare no ill will towards you
If you didn't lend a hand
But I'll always lift you up
If you had time to sit with me
I remember all you've done for me
Acts that are so grand or so small
Even if my mind forgets
My heart will remember them all

Be Free

I find myself surrounded in silence
And buried deep in darkness
Yet burdened with visions
And voices that are not my own
Listening to stories of woe
And seeing pain in hearts
People struggling to live
While fighting hatred and fears
Trying to find love abound
Spreading peace and joy
Helping others without reward
Simply doing what is right
This is how to banish darkness
And it's the only cure for silence
So remember these words
No matter how faint or loud
Things are not yet over
And for that you should be proud
So continue to live your life
And always be the best you can be

Hidden Charm

She hid her heart away years ago
Buried it deep in the ground
Protected by a strong box
Bound and sealed forever
But that doesn't stop me
From going after it
To return that great gift
This quest I must win
Following the clues for years
The search rages on
Digging through forgotten past
I finally find my reward
The box is now with its owner
She opens it to see what's inside
But is shocked at what she sees
Nothing inside but how
I think it's easy to see
She's had it all along

Jaded Lines

Remember those words I wrote to you
Oh so many years ago
The pages are no longer white
Blue lines long faded away
The ink has swelled and blurred
Stains now seem so clear
Try as I might those words are gone
Lost to me forever in time
No I don't remember them anymore
But I still know what they meant
Every pen stroke was a letter
Saying how much I love you
But those days are long gone now
And you have since move on
Yet these words I know are true
No matter what I will always love you

Calvin Warden II

My family tell me one thing thing
But my friend say another

Why

The school teaches me this
Religion tells me that

Why

The news seems incomplete
And the myths sound so real

Why

You have your own truth
But theirs is so different

Why

I want to believe your words
But I have so many questions

Why

My heart tells me one thing
My mind is saying no

Why

Your truth their truth my truth
But none of it is the real truth

Why

The more we know
The less we understand

Why

Truth is simply what is
And not what we perceive

That's why

Spread Truth

They made fun of me
For singing my song of peace
Calling me a crazy loon
Because I believe in love
Laughed as I traveled
Spreading joy to the world
But I pay them no mind
Caring not for your thought
Just living my life
Ignoring all their hate
Doing the best I can
Trying to heal everywhere I go
Teaching others the truth
Showing that it's not to late
Together we can all be family

The Artist

Up all night
Staring at the blank page
Seeing the image so clear
Hearing all the words
Know they want to come out
But unable to write
Feeling so many emotions
Lost In the story
Trying to find the style
Only to come up empty
How does this want to be told
As a story so long
Images drawn so clean
A poem of words
Or some other form
Fading as frustration sets in
Dreaming of the blank page
Seeing the flurry of untold art
Waking to silent images gone
And yet the work is done
The story has now been told
The artist's work is never done

Watching and Waiting

I sit alone watching the clouds gather
Growing in size and getting darker
Waiting for what I know is about to happen
Then with a flash and bang it begins
The sky falls and refreshes the world
Washing away all the sorrow and tears
Though the thunder booms
And the lightning continues
I still sit here looking up to the sky
Alone I watch as the rain falls
And washes over me again
Now I'm refreshed and renewed
And the storm moves on
All that's left is to wait and see
What will flourish in its wake

In The Sky

In the sky I wish to fly
No one could hear me cry
Everyone would let me be
As I soar up here free
This time is over
We now need a lover
My friends the time has come
We'll join to become one
For we lived the game
The beast is tamed
The game has come to an end
Together I stand with a friend
My love had finally come
I'm no longer in pain

Free But Alone

It was a hot summer night
The moon was bright
I could see the rejection
It was all over your face
The pain like a dull knife
Is inflicted upon me
I'll hide in outer space
'Cause I know it's a let down
Don't tell me anymore
It's the rejection I see
I'm free but I'm alone
Love is on its way
It needs to find me
Love will set me free

Sixteen

I was sixteen when I lost her
She was my friend but more
She was my woman
And I loved her so

Now she's gone I miss her so
She kissed me and walked out the door
She left me a lonely man
But I had to let her go

She was my first love
To whom I adore
But now I'm a better man
I still love her so

In Search Of Her

I have seen her a million times
I've wanted to hold her so many times
I see her when she's all alone
Every night I follow her home
I see the pain she goes through
I know it's true all too true
Everyone feels this way
But not everyday
I can't live without her anymore
I try saying these words the right way
Searching for the words day after day

All in a Dream

To see the beauty of sleep
As we all search for love
For some it's only a dream
Others the only way of life
As our sleep grows deeper
I must know right now
What do you hope to see
Protector's Soul

You asked me why I do what I do
A simple question I cannot answer
Helping you through the pain
Showing you there's another way
The journey we share may be flawed
But together we seem to carry on
I may lean on you sometimes
But I'll be there in times of need
Showing you that I care
Without saying a word aloud
Proving that I'll always love you
Because of what I have
Because of who I am
This is what I share with you

Protector's Soul

You asked me why I do what I do
A simple question I cannot answer
Helping you through the pain
Showing you there's another way
The journey we share may be flawed
But together we seem to carry on
I may lean on you sometimes
But I'll be there in times of need
Showing you that I care
Without saying a word aloud
Proving that I'll always love you
Because of what I have
Because of who I am
This is what I share with you

The Fool, Me

To know the pain she feels
She talks to me, "The Fool"
Not her but me
I know how she feels
Lost alone and afraid
So out of place
As if from another time
To join this strange (human) race
See the fool on the hill
I said to introduce myself
Yet it's but a dream
'Cause in the walking hour
Their sight of her is gone
"The Fool" is still me

Calvin Warden II

The Fool Within

We all search for the fool
The fool hidden in solitude
Searching through the valleys
The abyss of every sea
To the heights of every heaven
Just to find the fool
It's easier then though
Look in the depths of my soul
The fool is within me

Powerful Love

I watch as you lie awake
In your state of confusion
While my love is strong for you
I stand speechless like a fool
I'll help you win his love
And I'll never tell you why
One day I'll leave this place
Then you'll realize why
You don't understand me
That is easy to see
I love you more than ever
I'll help you win his love
Just remember one thing
ME

Empty Tether

I've seen the terror
Caused by an empty heart
I've known the fear
Which comes when you're alone
You think your world is falling
Through empty space and time
Reach out and catch my hand
I'm here to help others like me
I'll feed your love so
Our love will grow strong

Inside These Walls

To see me is confusing
To know me is strange
The appearance of a madman
The soul of loneliness
To live in chaos
To fear this life
Some call me a joker
Some know my cover
No one to handle me
These four walls contain me
These thoughts destroy me
These walls stop her and now
Tear down these walls

Dream

I'm looking in this room
Serving for salvation
I'm looking for her love
Only she can save me
I'll know her when
When time is right
The dreams will say
The Dream Master knows
And will guide me true
My heart will let me know.

Dreamland

I'm aware of this state of mind
This strange land I have entered
It's known as a dreamscape
What happens when it's up to me
I could have my worst dreams
Or even my worst nightmare
I've seen an angel change form
Till it was a deadly snake
All in the blink of an eye
The one thing I have yet to achieve
Is to win love that's as true as you
I spent my time looking for your love
All the time holding from lady death
I pray that I find you soon

Holding in a Dream

Give me a kiss my love
I need to know you're true
I want to hold your heart
Hold it deep in my soul
Look long into my eyes
You'll see my fear is true
I fear to get closer to you
My fear is strong as you know
But I need you more than ever
So I'll hold you in my dreams

Blind Path

I find myself standing in the crossroads
Not sure where I'm going
Can't tell where I've been
Trying to decide where to go
But I haven't got a clue
Will I continue to go forward
Go back from whence I came
Or will life take a drastic turn
Here I stand lost and alone
Spinning round and round
Searching for a sign
Trying to determine which way to go
And see if I can even take a step
As the world stops spinning
I begin to stumble and fall
Taking a step I now know
The path has been chosen for me
But where will it lead me
And who I will meet on this journey
I know not these answers
But I for one, can't wait to see

Part Of You

You ask for the moon
I say no
You ask for the sun
I say no
You ask for the universe
I say no
What will you give me then
You asked
I will give you everything
I replied
But when I ask you
You say no
But those thing I cannot give
Don't you see
For the things that you ask for
Are part of you
I can not take from your parts
To make you whole

Isolation Destroys

Sitting alone I find myself lost
Listening to the silence scream
And watching shadows in the dark
Wondering how I got here
Not even knowing where I am
And no clues as to where I've been
Is this self imposed isolation
A way to find myself once again
Or was I left with no choice
Was it something that I did
Or maybe something I said
Was I in over my head
Whatever their cause may be
The results are crystal clear
And I know what I have to do
I must break through this wall
The one that surrounds me alone
And face the world once again

To Whom It May Concern

These words I write for you
The one I've yet to meet
You know that I love you
And I've been waiting here
Seeing visions of you
Though I've gone blind
Answering your call
With words I don't speak
Listening to your voice
In deafening silence
So how do I know you're true
And not just a dream
Because I have so much love
And it's just waiting for you

In The Name of Friendship

When I look in your eyes I see your fear
I can tell your heart is empty
As you look for comfort in me
I'll help you every way I know how
'Cause my friendship is strong
But now your soul has grown weak
I'll share my love with you
So your heart will grow
I'll tell you nothing but the truth
I expect little in exchange
Your friendship is all I need

I've seen the future in your eyes
I've seen the changes in the world
You know the importance of your life
You know what you mean to me
My love is strong that is true
My love is gladly shared with you

Fear

As I look deep into your eyes
I see the fear boiling up within
You feel so distant to me
Your love has created a new fear
Look deep into your heart
Do away with unnecessary fear
I don't wish to hurt you
And you know that's true
I'll help banish your fear
Just keep your mind clear
I'll enter you heart
And take away your fear

Don't Judge Me

Don't judge me
If you don't know me
Don't ignore me
You don't know what I have to say
Don't trash me
Because of the way I look
Don't dismiss me
Due to the way I act
Don't shut me out altogether
You don't know my worth
I won't put you down
Cause you are not me

Sometimes A Man Can Bleed

My dreams are always changing
In the past they were nightmares
But now they have changed
My dreams are about love
And the time we were together
I know we won't get back together
But I still hold the dreams
They're locked away in my heart
Everyone said I should leave town
But it's not me they're putting down
I've been shoved and pushed around
You drove my life right into the ground
You know what you've done to me
And you don't seem to care
And with all you've put me through
I still love you

Understand Me

I once had a friend
She was very dear to me
Held a special place in my heart
But something happened
Things have changed
I don't even know her now
I couldn't take it anymore
So I gave her a tearful goodbye
She just stood confused
Finally she spoke up
Asked what she said wrong
I just turned away and walked
She demanded an answer
And memories flooded my head
You don't understand my dear
For it's not what you have said
You weren't there in my need
Many calls left unanswered
Messages with no reply
And yes I will always love you
But I leave not for what was said
But for all the things left unsaid

Remember Me

If I went missing today
Would you search for me
Or would you think I ran away
Believing lies of a dangerous life
And those who say I don't care
Questioning my family bonds
And my resolve to make it better
Know that life has been tough
Would you think I just gave up
In your heart you know the truth
Knowing that I always push through
And family means everything to me
So why do you turn your back
I think I understand now
It's not that you don't know
It's just easier to accept the lies
After all my skin doesn't fit in
Well whatever is your reason
REMEMBER ME!

Calvin Warden II

Stand Together

I stand for justice and equality
Through love, peace and harmony
I care not about race, sex, or orientation
Nor you age, appearance, or religion
I will not judge or belittle you
So just be the the real you
As long as you do no harm
I'll answer your call to alarm
I am not a trader to my own kind
And there is no guilt in my mind
My race is human
And love my religion

Sadness's Tears

There is hatred in the air
Terror fills our streets
Everyone seems so mad
There's no peace to be found
People fighting a cause
Others just starting chaos
When will people learn
We all need to get along
Forget our differences
Embrace who we are
Open our eyes and see
What every child sees
Hate is something learned
But love comes naturally
So stop all the fighting
And accept that we are one

Rising Sun

I awake once again
Ready to face a new day
But I find myself unable to rise
Just sitting on the side of the bed
Bound by these senseless doubts
And unreasonable feelings of dread
All sense of reason has gone
I'm simply buried in my fears
No one else can see my problem
Or understand this invisible pain
Because there is no real reason
No cause for feeling this way
Caught in my own illusions
Living without really living
As tears run down my face
And years of life pass me by
I don't really want to live
Nor do I really want to die
Now I'm stuck in this limbo
Made up of my own thoughts
Not knowing what to do

Journal of a Lonely Man

Feeling so empty inside
Listening to my own demos
Not able to see the light
I call out for a moment's peace
A simple chance to catch my breath
I see all the loving people
Knowing not why they're there
They can't be there for me
I know I'm not worthy
But in my heart I know them
And I want to let them all in
But is it right to burden them
To spread my misery and pain
I feel I must carry the load alone
But then one by one they step
Each taking a piece from me
This I do not understand
How did they even find me
But now my family and friends
They have all begun to lift me
Raising up to face the sun
And the life I've forgotten
The warmth it's stirring
Something breaks free
I know it's a long journey
But once again I will be me

www.ingramcontent.com/pod-product-compliance
Lightning Source LLC
LaVergne TN
LVHW011843060526
838200LV00054B/4140